I believe in unicorns

a magical make-believe colouring book

I believe in unicorns
a magical make-believe colouring book

ISBN: 978-1-911219-60-6

Created by Christina Rose

Contributors: Letitia Clouden, Shutterstock

www.bellmackenzie.com

BELL & MACKENZIE
PUBLISHING LIMITED

I believe in unicorns

I believe in unicorns

 I believe in unicorns

I believe in unicorns

I believe in unicorns

I believe in unicorns

I believe in unicorns

I believe in unicorns

I believe in unicorns

I believe in unicorns

I believe in unicorns

I believe in unicorns

I believe in unicorns

I believe in unicorns

I believe in unicorns

I believe in unicorns

 I believe in unicorns

 I believe in unicorns

I believe in unicorns

I believe in unicorns

 I believe in unicorns

I believe in unicorns

I believe in unicorns

I believe in unicorns

I believe in unicorns

I believe in unicorns

 I believe in unicorns

I believe in unicorns

 I believe in unicorns

I believe in unicorns

I believe in unicorns

I believe in unicorns

I believe in unicorns

I believe in unicorns

 I believe in unicorns

I believe in unicorns

I believe in unicorns

 I believe in unicorns

I believe in unicorns

I believe in unicorns

I believe in unicorns

I believe in unicorns

I believe in unicorns

I believe in unicorns

Name: Emily

I believe in unicorns